God's
little book of
Encouragement

David Marshall

Dedicated to Jill

Introduction

*From time to time we could all do with a 'lift'.
Perhaps it was because He knew this, that God filled
His Book with words of encouragement.
The Gideons have brought encouragement to millions
by placing copies of God's Book in hotel and
guesthouse rooms in so many parts of the world.
This Little Book of Encouragement picks out those
verses which, over the centuries, have brought uplift
and power.*

David Marshall

All texts are taken from the New International Version,
unless otherwise stated.

First published in 2000 by
AUTUMN HOUSE
Grantham, Lincs, NG31 9SL

A catalogue record for this book is available from the British Library.

ISBN 1 873796 89 7
Reprinted 2001, 2004, 2006 and 2007

When all your friends have let you down, when no one can be trusted – there's One who will never betray your friendship.

When I am afraid, I will trust in you. In God, whose word I praise, in God I trust; I will not be afraid. What can mortal man do to me?

Psalm 56:3, 4

Fight fear with trust and, because God gives power upon request, joy is around the corner.

'Surely God is my salvation; I will trust and not be afraid. The Lord, the Lord, is my strength and my song; he has become my salvation. With joy you will draw water from the wells of salvation.'

Isaiah 12:2

When things look really bad, remember: God has surprises up His sleeve! God's surprises can turn things around – and scatter your enemies.

'So do not fear, for I am with you; do not be dismayed for I am your God. I will strengthen you and help you; I will uphold you with my righteous right hand. . . . All who rage against you will surely be ashamed and disgraced; . . . though you search for your enemies, you will not find them.'

Isaiah 41:10-12.

When the picture looks bleak
don't ask God to take you
out of it but to join you in it.
That way everything is
transformed, including you.

At the height of the storm
'[Jesus] got up, rebuked the
wind and said to the waves,
"Quiet! Be still!" Then the wind
died down and it was
completely calm.'

Mark 4:39

Your defences are down
and you feel depressed
and vulnerable?
Help is at hand.

The Lord is a refuge for the
oppressed, a stronghold in
times of trouble. Those who
know your name will trust in
you, for you, Lord, have never
forsaken those who seek you.

Psalm 9:9, 10

Caught in a corner with no way out? There *is* a way. . . .

Call upon me in the day of trouble; I will deliver you, and you will honour me.

Psalm 50:15

When you are buffeted
by the storms of life
and your decks are awash,
a change of captain
may be called for.

O Lord, you are my God; I will
exalt you and praise your
name, for in perfect
faithfulness you have done
marvellous things, things
planned long ago. . . . You have
been a refuge for the poor, a
refuge for the needy in his
distress, a shelter from the
storm and a shade from the
heat.

Isaiah 25:1, 4

Problems can
get out of proportion,
and not only in the
wee small hours.
Don't let the problems
eclipse the Master.
Let the Master
eclipse the problems.

If God is for us, who can be
against us? He who did not
spare his own Son, but gave
him up for us all – how will he
not also, along with him,
graciously give us all things?

Romans 8:31, 32

If you trust, you can be knocked down, but never knocked out. And even when you're knocked down, there's a strong arm to lift you up and a gentle hand to dust you off.

We are hard-pressed on all sides, but we are never frustrated; we are puzzled, but never in despair. We are persecuted, but never deserted: we may be knocked down but we are never knocked out!

2 Corinthians 4:8, 9, J. B. Phillips
The New Testament in Modern English

There is hope beyond failure.
There is success beyond
failure. God loves to rebuild a
'failure' – and will act
when asked.

My flesh and my heart may fail,
but God is the strength of my
heart and my portion for ever.

Psalm 73:26

When you are at your weakest and most impotent is when God is best able to make you a person of power.

' "My grace is sufficient for you, for my power is made perfect in weakness." '

2 Corinthians 12:9

We are three-dimensional:
body, mind and spirit. What
air is to the body and mind,
prayer is to the soul.

Be happy in your faith at all
times. Never stop praying.
Be thankful, whatever the
circumstances may be.
For this is the will of God
for you in Christ Jesus.

1 Thessalonians 5:16-18, Phillips

Prayer is not magic.
You don't have to know
key phrases that 'work'.
Prayer is the genuine pouring
out of the heart
to the Great Listener.

Pray at all times and on every
occasion in the power of the
Holy Spirit. Stay alert and be
persistent in your prayers. . . .

Ephesians 6:18, New Living Translation

Prayer does not twist
God's arm to give you
what you want,
but it puts you
in a frame of mind
to accept His will
for you.

In Gethsemane Jesus prayed:
'My Father, if it is not possible
for this cup to be taken away
unless I drink it, may your will
be done.'

Matthew 26:42

Feeling deserted
is just that:
a feeling.
God makes sure
that you are never
really deserted.
He is with you
in Person.

At my preliminary hearing
no one stood by me.
They all ran like scared rabbits.
But it doesn't matter –
the Master stood by me.

2 Timothy 4:16, 17, The Message
The New Testament in Contemporary
Language by Eugene H. Peterson

The people who
intimidate you,
who *are* they
when all is said
and done?
You have a Friend
in high places.

The Lord is my light and my
salvation – whom shall I fear?
The Lord is the stronghold of
my life – of whom shall I be
afraid?

Psalm 27:1

When we come to God
we can knock and enter.
We don't have to
go through a secretary
or submit to security checks.
We never get a busy tone
when we dial His number.
We are ushered directly
into His presence.

This resurrection life you
received from God is not a
timid, grave-tending life. It's
adventurously expectant,
greeting God with a childlike
'What's next, Papa?'

Romans 8:15, Message

Feeling lonely, afraid,
discouraged?
Lost your way, even
your address?
You have a Companion
who is warm and friendly.
He will guide you home.

Do not be afraid or
discouraged, for the Lord is the
one who goes before you. He
will be with you; he will neither
fail you nor forsake you.

Deuteronomy 31:8, NLT

Society may declare you
'redundant', of no further use
to the economy.
But society's attitude
to you does not
reflect God's attitude.
He has a plan
and a future for you.

In his heart a man plans his
course, but the Lord
determines his steps.

Proverbs 16:9

Always remember that, no matter what you are doing, you are 'on mission' for God, His representative in a gone-astray world.

Whatever your task is, put your whole heart and soul into it, as into work done for the Lord and not merely for men – knowing that your real reward will come from him.

Colossians 3:23, Phillips

When they insult
and outsmart you,
the Jesus response
is best.
Act, don't react.

When they hurled their insults
at him, he did not retaliate;
when he suffered, he made no
threats. Instead, he entrusted
himself to him who judges
justly.

1 Peter 2:23

Away from home and feeling lonely? Draw your strength from your roots. Remember your principles and stay loyal to them. Trust in God's reasoning, not your own.

Never let loyalty and kindness get away from you! Wear them like a necklace; write them deep within your heart. Then you will find favour with both God and people, and you will gain a good reputation.

Proverbs 3:3, 4, NLT

Don't fret about what
people think of you.
What God thinks
is what counts.
He has promised you
an inheritance.

Refrain from anger and turn
from wrath; do not fret – it
leads only to evil. For evil men
will be cut off, but those who
hope in the Lord will inherit
the land.

Psalm 37:8, 9

When you have problems
remember the Bible's words:
'It came to pass' – *not to stay*.
Hang in there!
A new day is dawning.

A little while, and the wicked
will be no more; though you
look for them, they will not be
found. But the meek will
inherit the land and enjoy great
peace.

Psalm 37:10, 11

People problems will not destroy you. In fact, if you react rightly, you can come out ahead.

'Love your enemies. Let them bring out the best in you, not the worst. When someone gives you a hard time, respond with the energies of prayer for that person. If someone slaps you in the face, stand there and take it. If someone grabs your shirt, giftwrap your best coat and make a present of it.'

Luke 6:26, 27, Message

If the stresses of life
make you sleepless,
there is a recipe for rest.
God offers rest through a
change of lifestyle – and
taking time out.

Jesus said, 'Come to me, all of
you who are weary and carry
heavy burdens, and I will
give you rest.'

Matthew 11:28, NLT

At a crossroads of life?
Check the signposts,
the compass and the map.
But, above all things,
talk to your Guide.

Trust in the Lord with all your
heart; do not depend on your
own understanding. Seek his
will in all you do, and he will
direct your paths.

Proverbs 3:5, 6, NLT

Do you sometimes
feel beyond the pale
of God's love, outside the
catchment area of
His salvation?
Yes? It's time to rejoice!

'It was the lost that the Son of
Man came to seek – and to
save.'

Luke 19:10, Phillips

**Does God seem
far away from you?
One of you moved.
And it wasn't Him.**

The Lord is near to all
who call on him,
to all who call on him
in truth.

Psalm 145:18

When sin closes in,
make a clean breast
of it with God.
Ask Him for
a heart transplant.

Hide your face from my sins
and blot out all my iniquity.
Create in me a pure heart,
O God, and renew a
steadfast spirit within me.

Psalm 51:9, 10

You want to
triumph over weakness
and sin? You need
to renew your relationship
with God.
Whatever your sin is,
it has hurt *Him*.

For I know my transgressions,
and my sin is always before me.
Against you, you only, have
I sinned and done what is
evil in your sight.

Psalm 51:3, 4

Even if you take a
thousand steps from God,
you only have to turn
around and take one step
back towards Him, because
He has followed
you all the way.

Have mercy on me, O God,
according to your unfailing
love; according to your great
compassion blot out my
transgressions. Wash away all
my iniquity and cleanse me
from my sin.

Psalm 51:1, 2

The greatness of a
person's power
is the measure of his
or her surrender.

As far as the east is from the
west, so far has he removed
our transgressions from us.

Psalm 103:12

To purify our hearts
there is just one thing
we have to do:
detach ourselves from
creatures and abandon
ourselves entirely to
the Creator.

He who conceals his sins does
not prosper, but whoever
confesses and renounces them
finds mercy.

Proverbs 28:13

The Bible's clearest portrait of God is as a Father with outstretched arms running to give returning wastrels a hug.

'While he was still a long way off, his father saw him and was filled with compassion for him; he ran to his son, threw his arms around him and kissed him. . . . The father said to his servants, "Quick! Bring the best robe and put it on him. . . . For this son of mine was dead and is alive again; he was lost and is found." '

Luke 15:20, 22, 24

When we're one of a group
of people who believe in a
God of pure goodness, we
are under an obligation to be
like Him.

God is light; in him there is no
darkness at all. If we claim to
have fellowship with him yet
walk in the darkness, we lie
and do not live by the truth.

1 John 1:5, 6

To live Christ's way
is to shine a floodlight
of hope into a valley
of darkness.

The darkness is passing and the
true light is already shining.
Anyone who claims to be in the
light but hates his brother
is still in the darkness.

1 John 1:8, 9

We can accept what Christ
has done without knowing
how it works; we certainly
will not know how it works
until we've accepted it.

God made him who had no sin
to be sin for us, so that in him
we might become the
righteousness of God.

2 Corinthians 5:21

The first step to salvation is to say, True, this is my situation at the moment; but my hand is outstretched to accept whatever a loving Father sends.

All have sinned and fall short of the glory of God, and are justified freely by his grace through the redemption that came by Christ Jesus.

Romans 3:23, 24

People are not saved by the number of Brownie points they have clocked up; but because Jesus died for their sins.

I consider everything a loss compared to the surpassing greatness of knowing Christ Jesus my Lord, . . . I consider them rubbish, that I may gain Christ and be found in him, not having a righteousness of my own that comes from the law, but that which is through faith in Christ – the righteousness that comes from God and is by faith.

Philippians 3:8, 9

Happy people rarely think about happiness. They're too busy losing their lives in service for others.

'There is no greater love than this – that a man should lay down his life for his friends.'

John 15:13, Phillips

Christ is the root of our salvation. Good works are the fruit of our salvation.

'I am the vine; you are the branches. If a man remains in me and I in him, he will bear much fruit; apart from me you can do nothing.'

John 15:5

There is no such thing
as a fate that falls on men
however they act; but
there is a fate that falls on
men *unless* they act.

They crucified him, and parted
his garments, casting lots: . . .
And sitting down they watched
him there.

Matthew 27:35, 36, King James Version

Take up the cross *He* sends, not a cross of your own construction.

Jesus said to his disciples, 'If anyone would come after me, he must deny himself and take up his cross and follow me.'

Matthew 16:24

There is no education
like adversity;
no university
like the school
of hard knocks.

What I do thou knowest not
now; but thou shalt know
hereafter.

John 13:7, KJV

Adversity is the diamond dust heaven polishes its jewels with.

I have laboured and toiled and have often gone without sleep; I have known hunger and thirst and have often gone without food; . . . If I must boast, I will boast of the things that show my weakness.

2 Corinthians 11:27, 30

God recruits
His best soldiers
in the highlands
of affliction.

This calls for patient endurance
on the part of the saints who
obey God's commandments and
remain faithful to Jesus.

Revelation 14:12

The majority of
the world's troubles
are caused by people
wanting to be
more important.

'When you give a banquet,
invite the poor, the crippled,
the lame, the blind, and you
will be blessed. Although they
cannot repay you, you will be
repaid at the resurrection of
the righteous.'

Luke 14:13, 14

Some of the worries
we have we should
not ask God
to take away,
but to forgive.

'Seek first [God's] kingdom and
his righteousness, and all these
things will be given to you as
well. Therefore do not worry
about tomorrow, for tomorrow
will worry about itself. Each
day has enough trouble of its
own.'

Matthew 6:33, 34

Science has found
a cure for most ills;
but it has found
no remedy for
the worst of them
– apathy.

'Whatever you did for one of
the least of these brothers of
mine, you did for me.'

Matthew 25:40

When God pardons,
He consigns
the offence to
the fathomless deeps
of everlasting
forgetfulness.

You will tread our sins
underfoot and hurl all our
iniquities into the depths of
the sea.

Micah 7:19

If you are
swept off your feet,
it's time to
get on your knees.

This is the assurance we have
in approaching God: that if we
ask anything according to his
will, he hears us.

1 John 5:14

The strength of our faith is
the strength of our prayer.
The strength of our hope is
the strength of our prayer.
The warmth of our love is
the warmth of our prayer.

Praise be to God, who has not
rejected my prayer or withheld
his love from me!

Psalm 66:20

The secret of
effective prayer
is knowing
how to
'let go and
let God'.

'Ask and it will be given to you;
seek and you will find;
knock and the door will be
opened to you.'

Luke 11:9

Prayer enlarges the heart
until it is big enough
to contain God's gift
of Himself.

'I will do whatever you ask in
my name, so that the Son may
bring glory to the Father.'

John 14:13

A prayerless
seven days
makes one weak.

Is any one of you in trouble?
He should pray. Is anyone
happy? Let him sing songs of
praise. . . . The prayer of a
righteous man is powerful and
effective.

James 5:13-16

A proud man looks down on everything and everyone. That is why he does not see the One above.

Praise and exalt and glorify the King of heaven, because everything he does is right and all his ways are just. And those who walk in pride he is able to humble.

Daniel 4:37

God gives spiritual food
to everyone – except
those who are full
of themselves.

Pride goes before destruction,
a haughty spirit before a fall.

Proverbs 16:18

God keeps His promises –
even when the circumstances
make it appear unlikely
that He will.

[Jesus] is the Yes pronounced
upon God's promises,
every one of them.

2 Corinthians 1:20, The New English Bible

Commit your past to the forgiveness of God, commit your present to the love of God, commit your future to the providence of God.

'Don't let this throw you. You trust God, don't you? Trust me. There is plenty of room for you in my Father's home. . . . And if I'm on my way to get your room ready, I'll come back and get you so you can live where I live.'

John 14:1, 3, Message

God has plans for *the* future
and *your* future.
Without those plans
the world would be
a maze without a clue.

He who testifies to all these
things says it again: 'I'm on my
way! I'll be there soon!'
Yes! Come, [Lord] Jesus!
The grace of the [Lord] Jesus be
with you all. Oh, Yes!

Revelation 22:21, Message

Do we have the courage to believe the promise that Christ will move the rocks that entomb us and set us free? Yes! He's done it before! He arose!

Christ rose first; then when Christ comes back, all his people will become alive again.

1 Corinthians 15:23, Living Bible

God is good.
God is faithful.
God is changeless.
So what is there
to worry about?

The Lord is good, a refuge in
times of trouble. He cares for
those who trust in him.

Nahum 1:7

God gives no guarantee that trouble will not strike His friends. What he *does* guarantee is to be with them – 'a tower of strength' – in their troubles.

'When you pass through the waters, I will be with you; when you pass through the rivers, they will not sweep over you. When you walk through the fire, you will not be burned; . . . For I am the Lord, your God.'

Isaiah 43:2, 3

When the current threatens to sweep you away, stand on the rock.

I call as my heart grows faint; lead me to the rock that is higher than I. For you have been my refuge, a strong tower against the foe.

Psalm 61:2, 3

There is safety, strength and warmth in shadow.

Because you are my help, I sing
in the shadow of your wings.
I stay close to you;
your right hand
upholds me.

Psalm 63:7

Troubles are inevitable.
Misery is optional.
The other option is joy.

I thank my God every time I
remember you. In all my
prayers for all of you, I always
pray with joy . . . being
confident of this, that he who
began a good work in you will
carry it on to completion until
the day of Christ Jesus.

Philippians 1:3-6

Your life is without a true foundation if, when you are faced with choices, you make up your own mind without consulting Him.

Whether you turn to the right or to the left, your ears will hear a voice behind you, saying, 'This is the way; walk in it.'

Isaiah 30:21

You would worry less about
what others think of you
if you realized
how seldom they do.
Cultivate *God's*
good opinion.

Let each carpenter who comes
on the job take care to build
on the foundation! Remember,
there is only one foundation,
the one already laid:
Jesus Christ.

1 Corinthians 3:10, 11, Message

Beyond all the pleasures
our senses can give,
there's still an adventure
waiting. Life has much
more to offer than
four score years
and a retirement home.

'No eye has seen,
no ear has heard,
no mind has conceived
what God has prepared
for those who love him.'

1 Corinthians 2:9

When we have conquered all known lands, accumulated all the possessions there are to be had, strolled on the finest beaches in the world and finally worked out how to programme the video recorder – what then?

Then I saw a new heaven and a new earth, for the first heaven and the first earth had passed away, and there was no longer any sea. I saw the Holy City, the new Jerusalem, coming down out of heaven from God. . . .

Revelation 21:1, 2

Is 'OK' as good as it gets?
Is this all there is?
When push comes to shove,
and the last party popper has
been popped – what then?

And I heard a loud voice from
the throne saying, 'Now the
dwelling of God is with men,
and he will live with them.
They will be his people, and
God himself will be with them
and be their God. He will wipe
every tear from their eyes.
There will be no more death or
mourning or crying or pain, for
the old order of things has
passed away.'

Revelation 21:3, 4

Gardens where weeds never grow. Streets where it's safe to be. Communities where everyone lives in harmony. That's how God has planned things.

He who was seated on the throne said, 'I am making everything new!' . . . He said to me: 'It is done. I am the Alpha and the Omega, the Beginning and the End. To him who is thirsty I will give to drink without cost from the spring of the water of life. He who overcomes will inherit all this.'

Revelation 21:5-7

There is a regulation
in the Royal Navy which says:
'No officer shall speak
discouragingly to another
officer in the discharge
of his duties.'

Blessed is he who has regard
for the weak; the Lord delivers
him in times of trouble. The
Lord will protect him and
preserve his life.

Psalm 41:1, 2

Criticism does much,
but encouragement
does more.
Encouragement
after criticism is
as the sun after
a shower.

The name of the Lord
is a strong tower;
the righteous run to it
and are safe.

Proverbs 18:10

We need encouragement
as much as crops need rain.
After we have received it,
we are in a position to
dish it out to others.

You are a shield around me,
O Lord;
my Glorious One,
who lifts up my head.
To the Lord I cry aloud,
and he answers me
from his holy hill.

Psalm 3:3, 4

The need to be appreciated is among the deepest cravings of human nature. You have it. Don't forget that others have it, too.

I lie down and sleep;
I wake again, because the
Lord sustains me.
I will not fear the tens of
thousands, drawn up against
me on every side.

Psalm 3:5, 6

The cynic says: 'Don't bother telling people your troubles. Half of them don't care, but the other half figure you probably had it coming.' Thank God cynics are in a minority!

God is our refuge and strength, an ever present help in trouble. Therefore we will not fear, though the earth give way and the mountains fall into the heart of the sea.

Psalm 46:1, 2

There are times when there are more questions than answers. At those times it is good to remember that faith is a gift. God gives it in proportion to our need.

It is by grace you have been saved, through faith – and this not from yourselves, it is the gift of God – not by works, so that no-one can boast.

Ephesians 2:8, 9

When you open the door to God, you will find that He already has His door wide open to you.

By entering through faith into what God has always wanted to do for us – set us right with him, make us fit for him – we have it all together with God because of our Master Jesus. And that's not all: We throw open our doors to God and discover at the same moment that he has already thrown open his door to us.

Romans 5:1-3, Message

There are times when the only thing to be done is to endure. While doing so it is best to fill one's mind and time as far as possible with the concerns of other people. It doesn't bring immediate peace, but it brings the dawn nearer.

Weeping may go on all night, but joy comes with the morning.

Psalm 30:5, NLT

Those who bring
sunshine to the lives
of others cannot
keep it from
themselves.

A happy heart makes
the face cheerful,
but heartache crushes
the spirit.

Proverbs 15:13

Suppose when we finally reach the top of a ladder we find it's leaning against the wrong wall?

There is a way that
seems right to a man
but in the end
it leads to death.

Proverbs 16:25

Too bad
that all the people
who know how
to run the country
are busy
driving taxi cabs
and cutting hair.

The lips of the righteous
nourish many,
but fools die for lack
of judgement.

Proverbs 10:21

Joy is the most infallible sign of the presence of God.

For the kingdom of God is not a matter of eating and drinking, but of righteousness, peace and joy in the Holy Spirit.

Romans 14:17

To be able to find joy
in another's joy,
that is the secret
of happiness.

The Spirit of the Sovereign
Lord is on me, because the
Lord has anointed me to
preach good news to the poor.
. . . And provide for those who
grieve in Zion – to bestow on
them a crown of beauty instead
of ashes, the oil of gladness
instead of mourning, and a
garment of praise instead of a
spirit of despair.

Isaiah 61:1-3

Joy is the
serious business
of heaven. And
it is only
a joyous love
that redeems.

'I tell you . . . there is more
rejoicing in heaven over one
sinner who repents than over
ninety-nine righteous persons
who do not need to repent.'

Luke 15:7

You cannot *choose* to have joy; though you can *choose* to have pleasure. However, once you have tasted joy, if both were in your power, you would never exchange it for the whole world.

The ransomed of the Lord will return. They will enter Zion with singing; everlasting joy will crown their heads. Gladness and joy will overtake them.

Isaiah 35:10

The surest mark
of a Christian
is not faith,
nor even love,
but joy.

May the God of hope fill you
with all joy and peace as you
trust in him, so that you may
overflow with hope by the
power of the Holy Spirit.

Romans 15:13

This is the secret of joy.
You no longer strive for your
own way; seek to achieve
your own salvation.
Instead, you accept God's
way, accept *His* salvation –
as the gift of His grace.

'My sheep listen to my voice; I
know them, and they follow
me. I give them eternal life,
and they shall never perish; no-
one can snatch them out of my
hand. My Father, who has given
them to me, is greater than all;
no-one can snatch them out of
my Father's hand.'

John 10:27-29

Joy and peace
cannot be had apart
from God Himself.
Like salvation,
they are a gift
of His grace.

'I tell you the truth, whoever
hears my word and believes
him who sent me has eternal
life and will not be condemned;
he has crossed over from death
to life.'

John 5:24

A joy transfusion is still the greatest need of most Christians. To have joy we must be 'in Christ'. To be 'in Christ' is to have the assurance of His salvation.

As long as we 'are in Christ Jesus', we are – Colossians 2:10 – 'complete in him' – every step of the way. As long as we are 'in Christ Jesus', we are – Ephesians 1:6 – 'accepted in the beloved', accepted because of Jesus. As long as we are 'in Christ Jesus', there is – Romans 8:1 – 'therefore now no condemnation'. (KJV.)

Belief is a truth
held in the mind.
Faith is a fire in the heart.

When people work, their wages
are not a gift. Workers earn
what they receive. But people
are declared righteous because
of their faith, not because of
their work.

Romans 4:4, 5, NLT

'Don't worry!'
Preposterous advice, surely!
Don't you have the
right to worry?
Knee deep in bills.
The family at odds.
The onset of aches
and pains. . . .

The Lord is near. Do not worry
about anything.

Philippians 4:5, 6,
New Revised Standard Version

We present our final trauma to God, as we have presented all the trials and tribulations we have suffered along the way.

It was now about the sixth hour, and darkness came over the whole land until the ninth hour.
. . . Jesus called out with a loud voice, 'Father, into your hands I commit my spirit.'

Luke 23:44-46

Because Jesus endured the
darkness and came through,
even the darkest tunnel
has its exit and every
bad Friday is followed
by resurrection
'on the third day'.

About the ninth hour Jesus
cried out in a loud voice, . . .
'My God, my God, why have
you forsaken me?'

Matthew 27:46

**Because of God *we belong,*
we can feel secure –
regardless of difficulties.**

Know that the Lord is God.
It is he who made us,
and we are his;
we are his people,
the sheep of his pasture.

Psalm 100:3

Your life must be built on
bedrock – not soft soil
or shifting sand – and that
bedrock is the utter
dependability of God.

For the Lord is good and his
love endures for ever;
his faithfulness continues
through all generations.

Psalm 100:5

If we address God as children, it is because He tells us He is our Father. If we unburden ourselves upon Him, it is because He tells us He is our Friend.

'Come to me, all you who are weary and burdened, and I will give you rest. Take my yoke upon you and learn from me, for I am gentle and humble in heart, and you will find rest for your souls.'

Matthew 11:28, 29

We have a Father who is Sovereign over all. Because of this, all evil must pass through the sieve of His love and wisdom before it can strike us – *and then be forced to work together for our good.*

We know that God causes everything to work together for the good of those who love God and are called according to his purpose for them.

Romans 8:28, NLT

Few people think about the suffering that sin has caused God. Our world is a vast scene of misery that we dare not allow our minds to dwell upon for long. The burden would be too terrible. *Yet God feels it all.*

He was wounded and crushed for our sins. He was beaten that we might have peace. He was whipped, and we were healed!

Isaiah 53:5, 6, NLT

Is final victory possible?

I looked and there before me
was a great multitude that no-
one could count, from every
nation, tribe, people and
language, standing before the
throne and in front of the
Lamb. . . . And they cried out
in a loud voice: 'Salvation
belongs to our God, who sits
on the throne, and
to the Lamb.'

Revelation 7:9, 10

God wants us to be happy
and at peace. To live lives
like that we need
to be focused.

You will keep in perfect peace
him whose mind is steadfast,
because he trusts in you. Trust
in the Lord for ever, for the
Lord, the Lord, is the Rock
eternal.

Isaiah 26:3, 4

With God there is no
such thing as a mission
impossible. When He sends
you 'on mission' He makes
sure you have the means
to succeed.

'Nothing is impossible
with God.'

Luke 1:37

The ever-present company of your forever Friend.

'Surely I will be with you always, to the very end of the age.'

Matthew 28:20

Even in the midst of life's storms you can stand in the rays of the Sun of Righteousness.

The peace of God, which transcends all understanding, will guard your hearts and your minds in Christ Jesus.

Philippians 4:7

There is a bridge into the kingdom of God that all men and women must cross. The bridge is called Forgiveness. And forgiveness must be received from God, and given to others.

'If you forgive men when they sin against you, your heavenly Father will also forgive you.'

Matthew 6:14

'This above all' – you need
a shield. This shield is
impenetrable because it is
manufactured in heaven.

Take up the shield of faith,
with which you can extinguish
all the flaming arrows of
the evil one.

Ephesians 6:16

It has been said, 'You cannot kill time without injuring eternity.' However, when we return to God, He has a way of making up the wasted years.

'I will repay you for the years the locusts have eaten.'

Joel 2:25

**God is prepared
to protect us
against all kinds
of danger.**

You are my hiding place; you
will protect me from trouble
and surround me with songs of
deliverance.

Psalm 32:7

God is no man's debtor. He will make it up to you.

God is not unjust; he will not forget your work and the love you have shown him as you have helped his people and continue to help them.

Hebrews 6:10

If you ask for his presence,
God is prepared to be your
forever Companion –
wherever you go, at all times.

Be strong and courageous.
Do not be terrified;
do not be discouraged,
for the Lord your God
will be with you
wherever you go.

Joshua 1:9

Even in our darkest times,
there are lessons to be
learned – and treasures
to be discovered.

'I will give you the treasures
of darkness, riches stored in
secret places, so that you may
know that I am the Lord,
the God of Israel, who
calls you by name.'

Isaiah 45:3

God's love and compassion
for you are fiercer, even, than
those of a mother for a
newborn baby.

'Can a mother forget the
baby at her breast and have no
compassion on the child
she has borne?
Though she may forget,
I will not forget you!'

Isaiah 49:15

No way can God ever forget
you. He carries your name
engraved on the palms of His
hands. Depend on it!

'See, I have engraved you on
the palms of my hands.'

Isaiah 49:16

This is no time to lose your nerve! Victory is within your grasp! Press on!

Do not throw away your confidence; it will be richly rewarded. You need to persevere so that when you have done the will of God, you will receive what he has promised.

Hebrews 10:35, 36

The world is a ship,
not an iceberg.
There is someone
at the controls;
it is not a runaway.

In just a very little while,
'He who is coming will come
and will not delay.
But my righteous one
will live by faith.'

Hebrews 10:37

There are anxious times for us all. There are times of weakness. But in those times God carries us.

Cast all your anxiety on him because he cares for you.

1 Peter 5:7

Walk in God's way, depend on God's blessing – and find yourself empowered.

The Lord your God will bless you in all your work and in everything you put your hand to.

Deuteronomy 15:10

We may tire, grow weary, stumble and fall. But if we depend on the Lord for strength we may yet soar.

Those who hope in the Lord will renew their strength. They will soar on wings like eagles; they will run and not grow weary, they will walk and not faint.

Isaiah 40:31

No committed Christian suffers from compassion fatigue. He knows that, just when the burden seems heaviest, the breakthrough is near.

Let us not become weary in doing good, for at the proper time we will reap a harvest if we do not give up.

Galatians 6:9

God sees to it
that a door
of opportunity
is always open
for the Christian.
If one door closes
it is because
another is about
to open.

'See, I have placed before
you an open door that
no-one can shut.'

Revelation 3:8

When death strikes close by, remember Jesus was not just resurrected, He *is* the resurrection and the life, and personally guarantees that those who die committed to His cause will live again.

'I am the resurrection and the life. He who believes in me will live, even though he dies; and whoever lives and believes in me will never die.'

John 11:25, 26

The arrogant may be insufferable, but their achievements are short-term. Only the humble know satisfaction at the personal level.

Once more the humble
will rejoice in the Lord;
the needy will rejoice in the
Holy One of Israel.

Isaiah 29:19

Anyone, any place,
any time, who comes to Jesus
is always, always, *always*
accepted. He saves to the
uttermost and the outermost.

He is able also to save them to
the uttermost that come unto
God by him.

Hebrews 7:25, KJV

There is a way back home for
every prodigal son
and daughter
no matter how 'backslidden'
they may consider
themselves to be.

'I will heal their waywardness
and love them freely, for my
anger has turned away
from them.'

Hosea 14:4